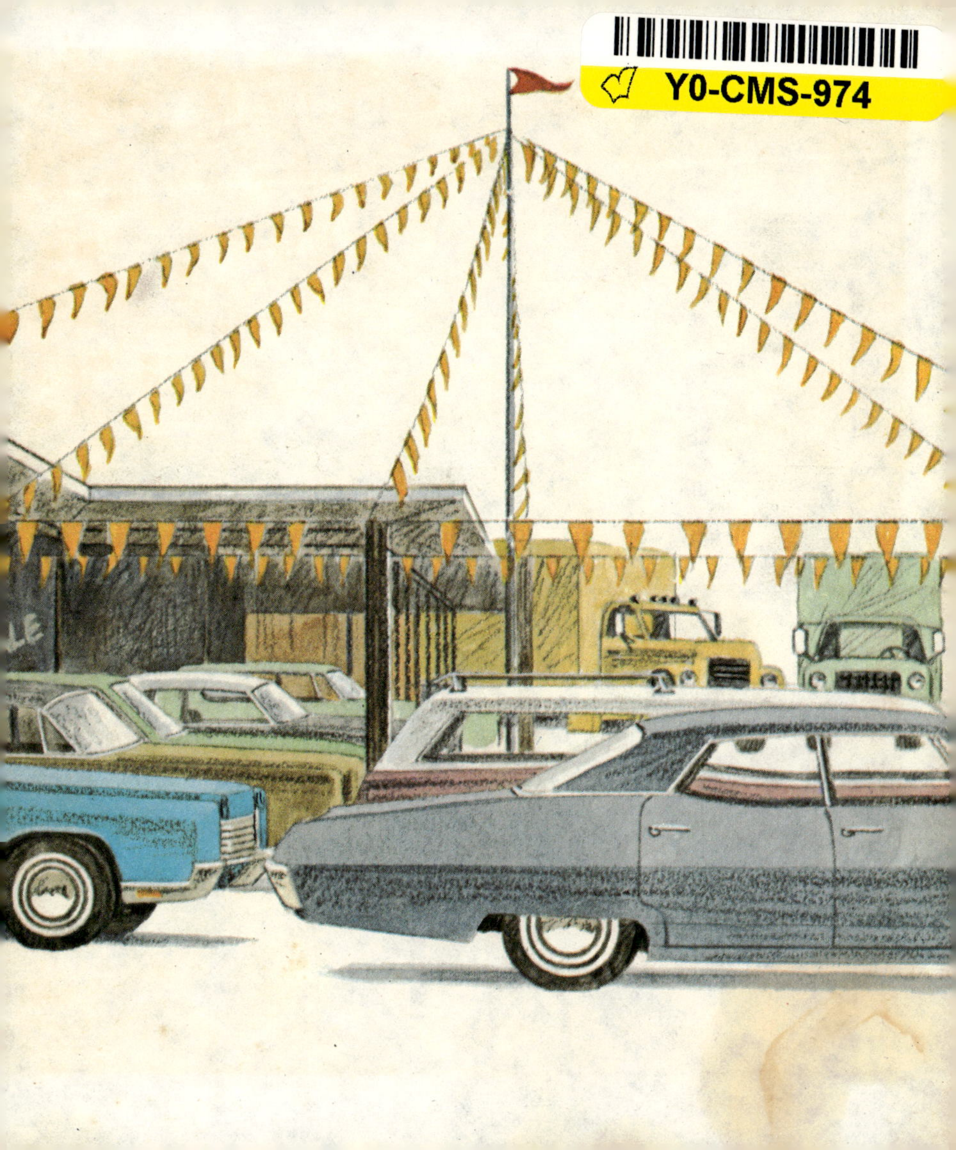

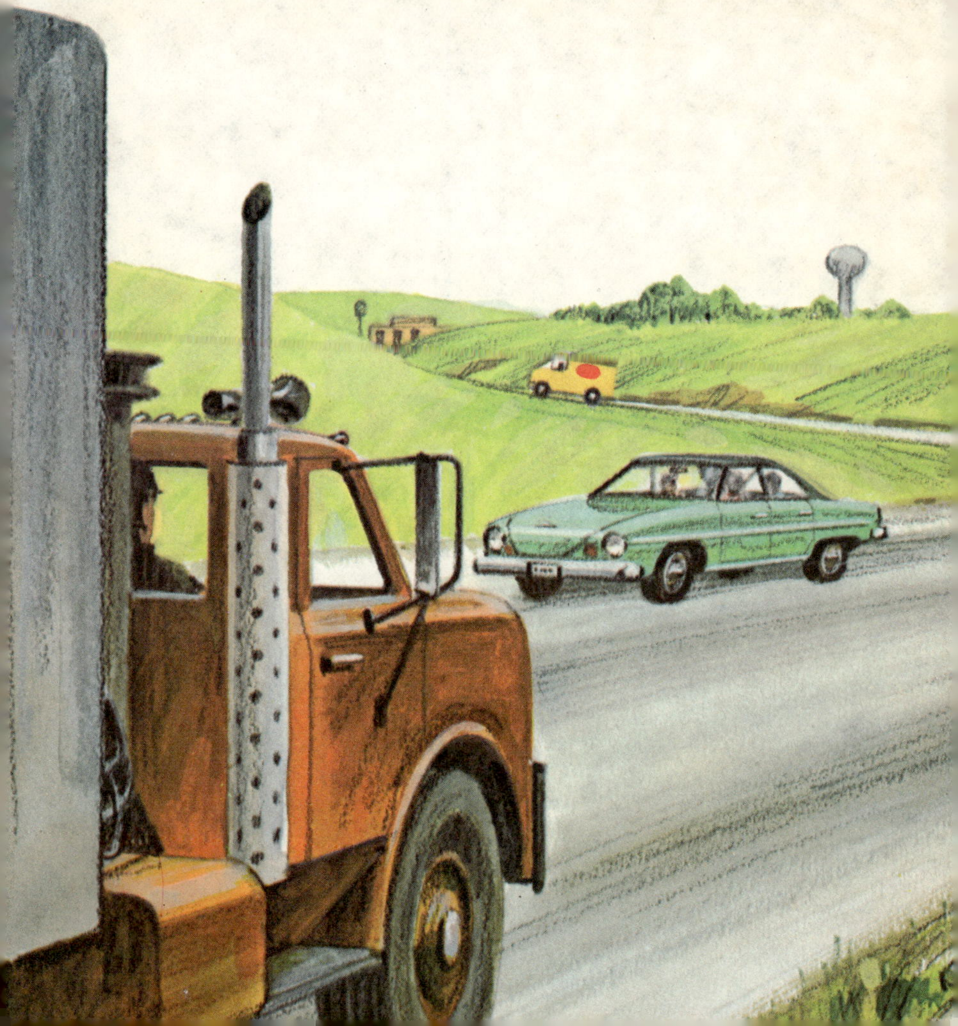

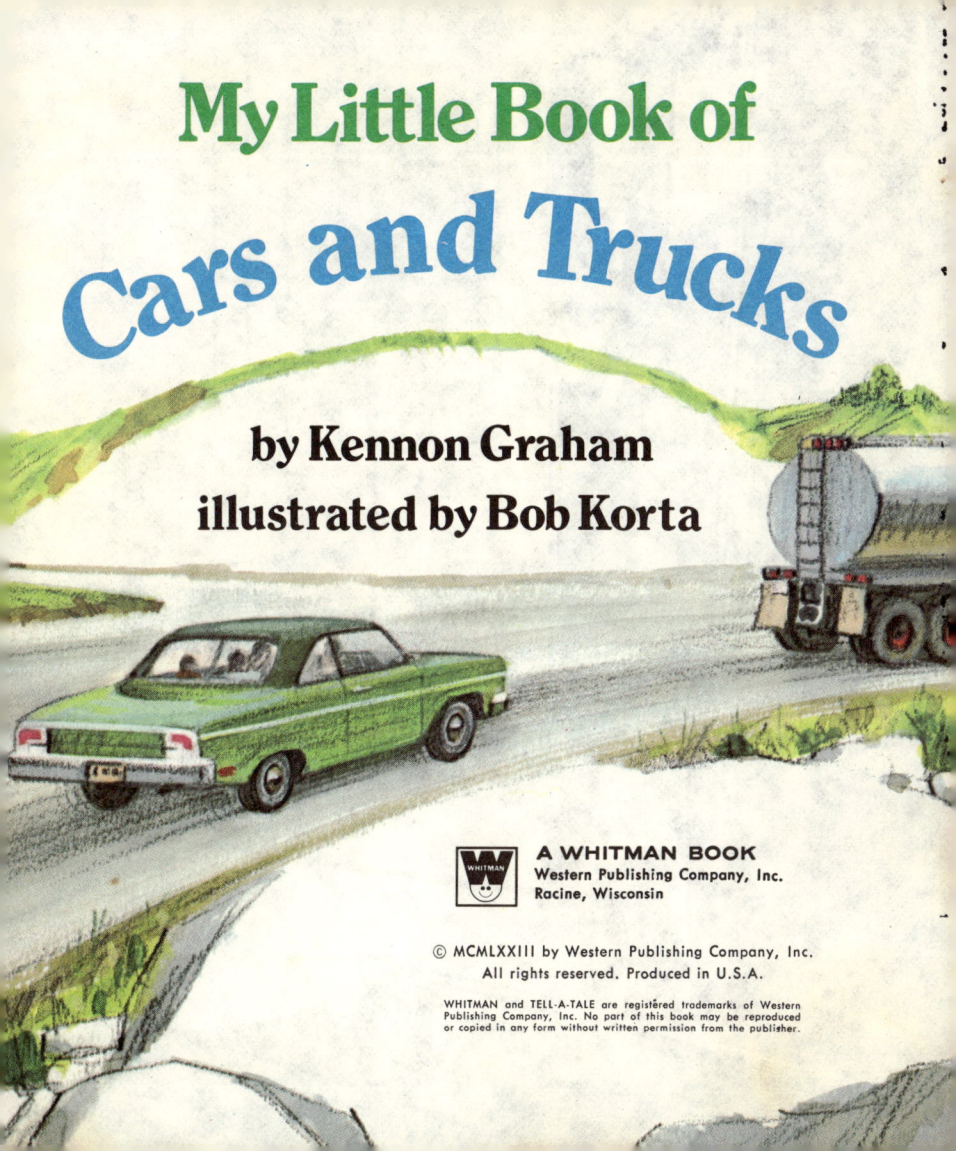

My Little Book of Cars and Trucks

by Kennon Graham

illustrated by Bob Korta

A WHITMAN BOOK
Western Publishing Company, Inc.
Racine, Wisconsin

© MCMLXXIII by Western Publishing Company, Inc.
All rights reserved. Produced in U.S.A.

WHITMAN and TELL-A-TALE are registered trademarks of Western Publishing Company, Inc. No part of this book may be reproduced or copied in any form without written permission from the publisher.

Cars and trucks,
Trucks and cars,
Everywhere you go.
Some small and very fast,
Some big and slow.

Some full of concrete,
Some full of bread,
Some painted black and white,
Some painted red.

Trucks that you can sleep in,
Trucks that carry fish,
Cars that drive you over sand
Or anywhere you wish.

Trucks that carry soldiers,
Trucks that carry dogs...

Trucks that carry criminals,
Trucks that carry hogs.

Trucks that carry loads of coal,
Cars that run in races,
Cars that take you on smooth roads

Or to bumpy, thumpy places.

Trucks that carry other trucks,
Trucks that carry pie,
Trucks that dig for water wells
Or raise their ladders high.

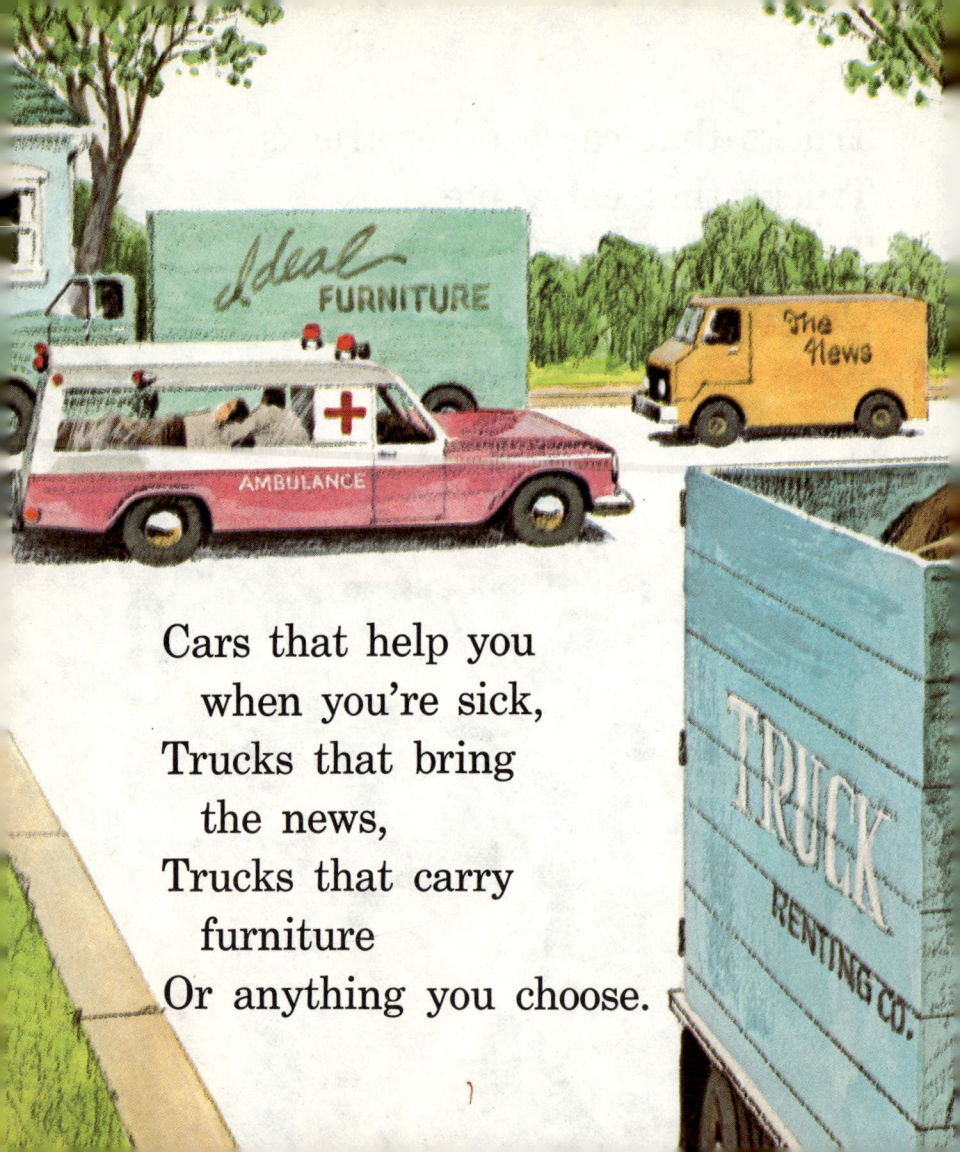

Cars that help you
  when you're sick,
Trucks that bring
  the news,
Trucks that carry
  furniture
Or anything you choose.

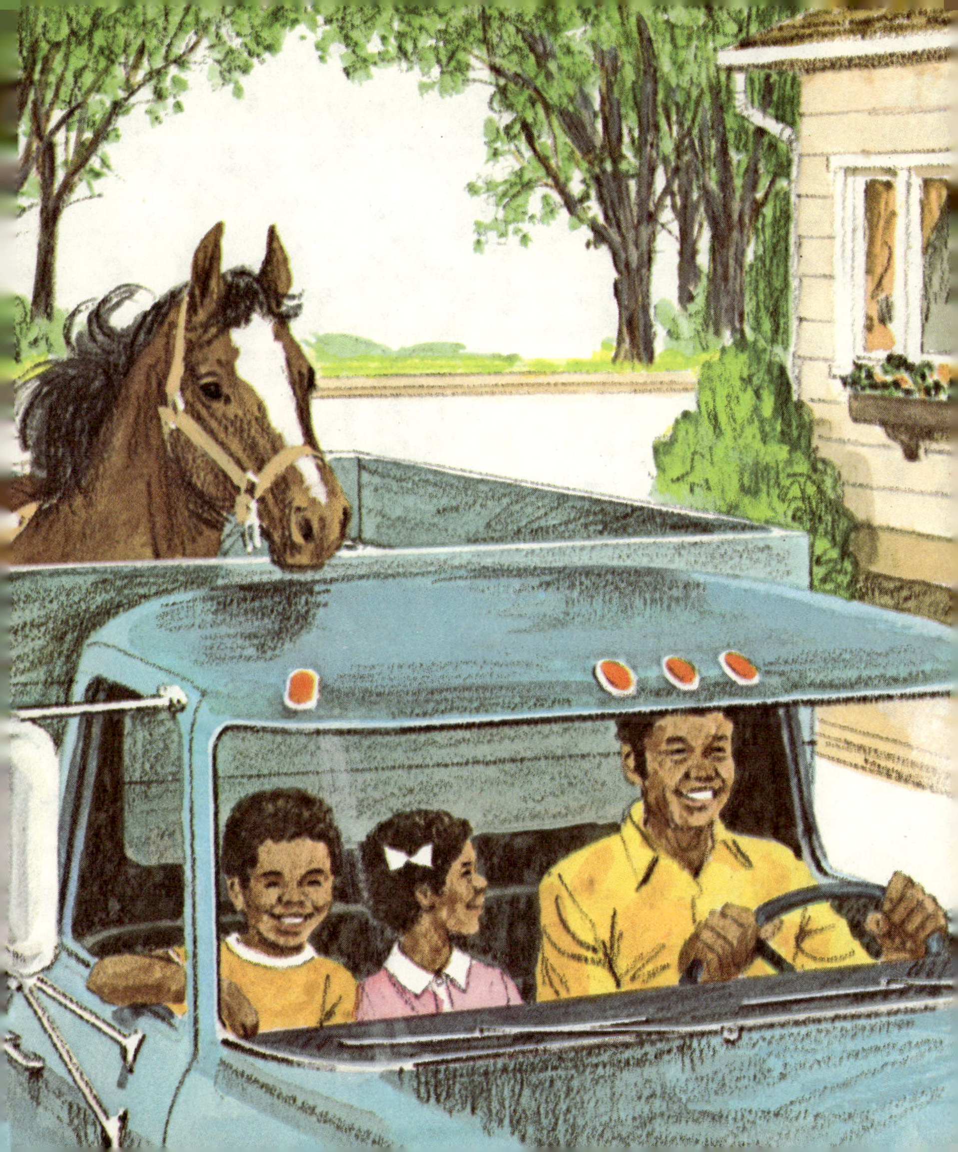

Cars and trucks,
Trucks and cars,
Some that carry honey . . .

Some that carry thirteen friends,

Some that carry money.

Trucks can haul your trash away;
Trucks can haul your car;
Trucks can haul your winter wood;
And trucks haul sticky tar.

Some deliver panes of glass;
Some deliver drapes;
Some deliver telephones;
And some deliver apes.

Cars with speakers on the roof,

Cars without a top . . .

DODGE'M

Cars that never travel far,
Cars that never stop.

Trucks that carry loads of butter,
Trucks that carry ice,

Trucks that carry loads of oranges,
Trucks that carry rice.

Some bring ice cream in the summer;
Some bring frosty pop;

Some bring in
 the farmer's milk;
Some bring in his crop.

Smaller cars with just two doors,
Larger cars with four,

Cars that make an awful screeching...

Cars that make a roar.

Some are full of packages;
Some are full of toys . . .

Some are full of sausage pizza;

Some are full of noise.

Big or little,
Old or new,
Fast or very slow,
Cars and trucks,
Trucks and cars...

They're always on the go!

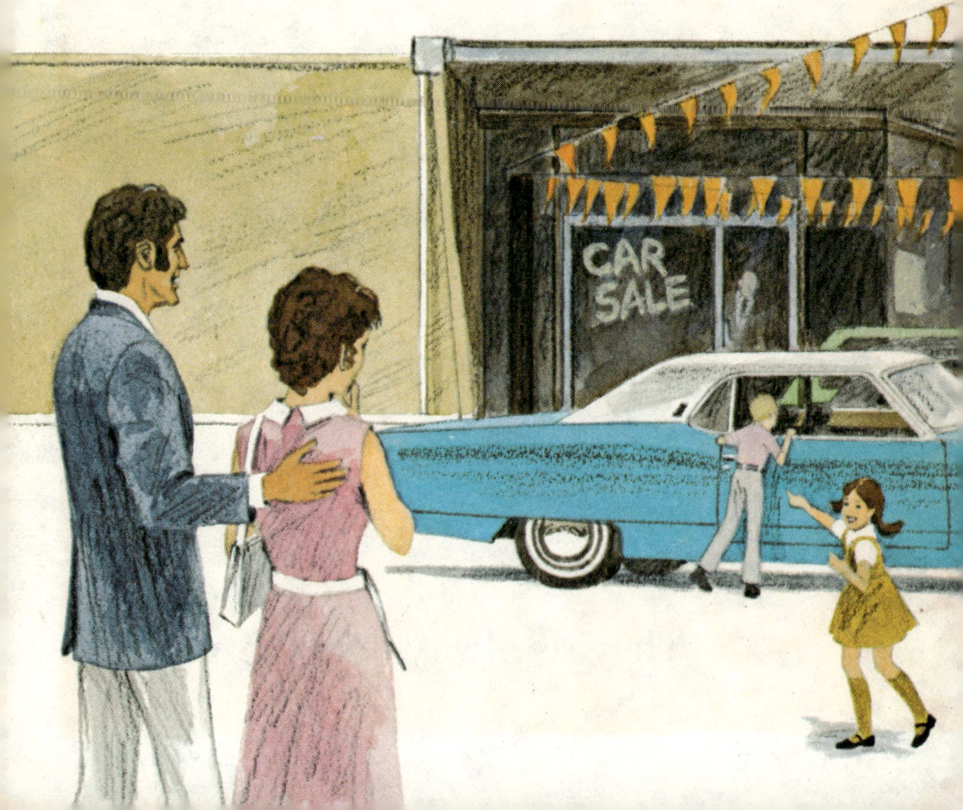
CAR
SALE